Down The Chimney

SHEPHERD KNAPP
[ZHINGOORA BOOKS]

Preface

This play is intended, not only for acting, but also for reading. It is so arranged that boys and girls can read it to themselves, just as they would read any other story. Even the stage directions and the descriptions of scenery are presented as a part of the narrative. At the same time, by the use of different styles of type, the speeches of the characters are clearly distinguished from the rest of the text, an arrangement which will be found convenient when parts are being memorized for acting.

The play has been acted more than once, and by different groups of people; sometimes on a stage equipped with footlights, curtain, and scenery; sometimes with barely any of these aids. Practical suggestions as to costumes, scenery, and some simple scenic effects will be found at the end of the play.

What sort of a Christmas play do the boys and girls like, and in what sort do we like to see them take part? It should be a play, surely, in which the dialogue is simple and natural, not stilted and artificial; one that seems like a bit of real life, and yet has plenty of fancy and imagination in it; one that suggests and helps to perpetuate some of the happy and wholesome customs of Christmas; above all, one that is pervaded by the Christmas spirit. I hope that this play does not entirely fail to meet these requirements.

Worcester, Mass.

SHEPHERD KNAPP.

Down the Chimney

The First Scene

Now the curtain opens, and you see the Roof of a House, just as Mother Goose promised. Keep your eyes open to see what will happen next, for here comes JACK FROST, *who is dressed all in white. He walks with a quick and nimble step, and this is what he says:*

Would you believe from the look of things, that to-morrow is Christmas? There is not a flake of snow anywhere. This roof is as clear as it is in summer. These pine trees, whose boughs hang over the roof, are all green. The chimney has not even an icicle on it. I hear people saying that we have no old-fashioned winters any more. Even old Mother Cary said to me the other day, "Jack Frost," said she, "when are you going to give them a real snow-storm?" But I told her not to be impatient: I would attend to it all in good time. And when I do begin, it doesn't take me long to get up a fine old storm, I can tell you. *Now he walks up to the Chimney, and knocks on the side of it.* Say, old fellow. *He waits a moment; then knocks again.* Wake up there. *He waits a moment; then knocks again.* Wake up, I say.

And now—would you believe it?—the Chimney opens, first, one of his eyes, then the other; and then his mouth and nose appear together. Each of his eyes is exactly the shape and size of one brick. So is his nose. And his mouth is as long as two bricks side

4

by side. They all turn a very bright red, when they appear, as though light were shining through them.

JACK FROST *goes on talking*: What do you mean, Mr. Chimney, by going to sleep in winter, I'd like to know? Summer is the time for you chimneys to go to sleep; but in winter when the people in the houses have their fires burning, you ought to keep wide awake, so as to carry off the smoke; don't you know that? Sleepy head! You ought to be ashamed of yourself.

THE CHIMNEY *answers*: Nothing of the sort. Have you forgotten what night this is, Jack Frost? Don't you know that this is Christmas Eve, when the fires are all put out, so that Santa Claus can climb down without getting burned? That's why I was taking a little nap. See? *He winks with one eye.*

JACK FROST *says*: Oh, that's it, is it? Well, that's true enough. I hadn't thought of old Santa Claus. He'll be here before long, probably.

Yes, too soon, *says* THE CHIMNEY; for I haven't had my sleep half out, and here you are, keeping me awake for nothing. With your kind permission, I'll take another forty winks.

And now his eyes close, then his nose and mouth disappear, and in a moment he is sound asleep again.

Lazy old fellow! *exclaims* JACK FROST. Well, I must get to work if we are to have a real old-fashioned storm before morning. And first for some wind. Where are those Wind Fairies, I wonder? They ought to be here by now. *He puts his hands beside his mouth, and calls in a high voice:* Hoo—oo! Hoo—oo!

THE WIND FAIRIES *are heard from far, far away, calling in answer:* Hoo-oo! Hoo-oo!

JACK FROST, *as soon as he hears them, says joyfully:* There they are. They'll be here in a second.

And now you can hear the Wind Fairies coming gradually nearer, making the wind-noise as the come, like this:

z—z—z   z—z—z   z—z—z—z—z—z—z
z—z—z z—z—z z z—z—z—z—z—z—z—z

This grows louder and louder, till suddenly in come the Wind Fairies, running. They are all in gray; they have on gray peaked caps, gray capes which comes down to their knees, and long gray stockings; and they have gray masks over the upper parts of their faces. The Fairies stop short before Jack Frost, and make him a low bow. Then they sing their song, which is called

THE SONG OF THE WIND FAIRIES1

Do you hear us blow, in our coats of gray?

Do you hear us blow, till the trees rock and sway?

Do you hear us blow—for from far, far away

We have come with a storm for your Christmas.

REFRAIN

Oh, the sound of the wind is strange for to hear;

And the breath of the wind, it is cold and clear;

You'll hear us blow, as we fly thro' the air,

And we've brought you a storm for your Christmas.

You can hear us sigh at the window-pane;

And we moan and cry in the snow and the rain.

Then away we fly, for we may not remain,

But we leave you a storm for your Christmas.

REFRAIN

Oh, the sound of the wind is strange for to hear;

And the breath of the wind, it is cold and clear;

You'll hear us blow, as we fly thro' the air,

And we've brought you a storm for your Christmas.

As soon as the song is over, off run the Wind Fairies, making the wind-noise as they go, which grows fainter and fainter as they get further and further away, like this

Z—Z—Z—z—z—z   z—z—z   z—z—z
Z—Z—Z—z—z—zz—z—zz—z—z

When the sound of the wind has quite died away, THE CHIMNEY opens one eye, and speaking slowly and sleepily, *says:* Look here, Jack, something's going on in my inside. *He opens the other eye, and his nose and mouth appear. He speaks more briskly:* It feels as though there were something hot in there. Do you suppose those stupid people in the house down below have forgotten all about Santa Claus, and are lighting the fire on the hearth? I believe they are. I wish you'd just climb up on my shoulder, and shout down to them to stop. Do: there's a good fellow.

JACK FROST *climbs up, puts his head over the chimney, then draws back coughing.* Fire? *cries he.* I should say there was, and smoke, too; enough to choke a locomotive. *He cautiously peers down.* Hello there, you people, put that fire out. Do you hear? Put it out. Santa Claus is coming. Do you hear what I say? SANTA CLAUS IS COMING. Put out that fire.

There is a pause; then a hissing sound, loud at first, then dying away, like this:

S—S—S—s—s—s—s—s—s

There! *says* JACK FROST, they've thrown a pitcherful of water on it. *He climbs down from the chimney.*

THE CHIMNEY, *who has now grown sleepy again, says to him, in a voice that grows fainter and fainter.* Thank you, my dear fellow: you—real—ly *(Here one eye closes)* are—ver—y—ki—*And he never finishes the sentence, for the other eye closes, and the nose and mouth "go out" at the same moment.*

Asleep again, I declare, *says* JACK FROST, *with disgust.* Well, now for the Snow Fairies.

He walks to the edge of the roof at one side, and blows a shrill blast on a whistle. Almost at once snow begins to fall from the sky, slowly at first, then more and more. Jack Frost looks up at it and nods his head approvingly. When it is snowing very hard, in come on tip-toe, very softly, the Snow Fairies, dressed in snowy white, with white hoods and muffs. Some of them quietly spread snow on the boughs of the trees, taking it out of their muffs; others hang flakes on the Chimney, in such a way as to make eyebrows, mustache, and beard for the face. But this doesn't show at first, because the Chimney is still asleep. Then the Fairies, standing in front of the Chimney, so that they hide it, sing their song, which is called

THE SONG OF THE SNOW FAIRIES2

When children go to bed at night,

We fairies come with snow-flakes white;

Cover the earth, silent and still;

House-top, and tree-top, and field and hill.

When children wake at morning light,

They find the world all snowy white.

Where, then, are we? Who of you know?

Cosily tucked in our beds of snow.

THE CHIMNEY, who is still hidden behind the Snow Fairies, wakes up while they are singing the last line, and calls out: What's this, I'd like to know? Who's been decorating my face?

The Snow Fairies stand back on either side, so that his face can now be seen, with its white eyebrows and mustache and beard, all made of snow-flakes; and he goes on talking in a jolly voice: Oh, you sly ones, you are at your old tricks. Well, well, I'm really glad to see you. It seems like old times to have snow at Christmas. Now don't mind me; go on with your work; cover me up with your snowflakes as much as you choose—eyes, nose, mouth, and all; I don't mind it a bit.

So the Snow Fairies, moving softly about, hang more snow-flakes on the chimney, even over his eyes and nose and mouth, which show dimly through the snow. His eyes blink now and then.

And now, sleigh-bells are heard in the distance.

Hark! cries JACK FROST.

They all listen: the bells are still heard, a little nearer.

Then JACK FROST continues: There comes Santa Claus, sure enough. Let's give the old fellow a surprise. Here! All hide behind the Chimney.

Very quickly, but very quietly, too, they all hide. The sleigh-bells come nearer and nearer, till they seem to be just outside: then they stop, and a voice, which plainly belongs to SANTA CLAUS, says: Whoa! Quiet, Prancer! Blitzen, stand still there!

And now Santa Claus himself appears, with his pack of toys. He walks to the middle of the roof, and sets down the pack.

It certainly is getting cold, says SANTA CLAUS to himself. For he does not see Jack Frost and the Snow Fairies, who are hidden behind the Chimney. He goes on talking: And what a lot of snow there is about here. It is really like the Christmas eves we used to have fifty years ago. My pack seems to be coming undone. He stoops to fix it. I should hate to have it burst open, while I was going down the Chimney.

Now the Snow Fairies have come out from behind the Chimney, and are stealing up behind him on tip-toe. When they are quite close, they throw great handfuls of snow at him. He starts up, surprised, but bursts into a great laugh:

Ho! ho! ho! This is a fine way to treat an old man! says SANTA CLAUS. Ho! ho! ho! ho! This is fine fun indeed! Hello, Jack Frost, is that you? And how are you, my little roley-poley snow-balls? White and light as ever, I see. And you've made me all white too, but not very light, I fear. Well, well, be off with you, for I must go down the Chimney.

He bows to the Chimney, whose eyes blink through the snow.

Good evening, my old friend, says SANTA CLAUS. YOU are enjoying good health, I hope. May I climb down inside of you as usual?

THE CHIMNEY answers, in a muffled voice, because he is so covered up with snow: Go ahead, Santa, I'm used to it.

So Santa Claus climbs to the top of the Chimney, steps over, and after throwing a kiss to the Snow Fairies, who return it, he goes down out of sight.

And that is the end of the First Scene.

THE INTERLUDE

Again, before the Second Scene begins, MOTHER GOOSE comes out in front of the curtain and this is what she says:

Well, my dears, I hope you are enjoying my little Play. And what do you suppose comes next? Wouldn't you like to see who lives down inside that house, where the chimney was; and what they were doing while Jack Frost and the others were up on the roof, and whether they heard the Wind Fairies; and whether they knew that the Snow Fairies had come; and how they came to make that mistake, lighting a fire in the fireplace where Santa Claus had come down? Well, that is just what the next scene is to be about. Last time we were up on the roof; this time we shall be down in the Room, in front of the fire-place. So be still and listen carefully, for now it is going to begin.

The Second Scene

When the curtain opens this time, you can see into the Room of the House, just as Mother Goose promised. Notice that on one side of the fire-place is a window with curtains drawn, on the other, a washstand with bowl and pitcher. In front, on right and left, are two large beds. In the middle of the room, with her back to the fire-place, the Grandmother is seated on a low chair, and about her in a half-circle on stools, sit the eight grandchildren, four girls and four boys, all in their night-clothes and wrappers.

ISABEL *begins by asking*: Grandmother, how old are you?

GRANDMOTHER *replies*: How old do you think, my dear?

ISABEL *guesses*: A hundred?

Almost, *says* GRANDMOTHER: Why, I can remember when all your mothers and fathers were little boys and girls like you. Your mother, Margaret and Sally, and your father, Jack and Tom and Helen, and your father, Isabel, and your mother, Ned and Frank, were my little boys and girls, you know; and on Christmas Eve I used to sit with them in the nursery, just as I am sitting with you now. That is why I told them to go downstairs and leave me alone with you for a little while tonight—for the sake of old times. Yes, they used to sit around me just like this, and then I used to tell them a story.

A story! A story! *cry* ALL THE CHILDREN.

And GRANDMOTHER says: Shall I tell you one? *The children all nod.* Let me think, *says she.*

The Wind Fairies are heard outside, making the wind-noise, like this:

z—z—z   z—z—z   z—z—z—z—z—z—z
z—z—z z—z—z z—z—z—z—z—z—z

GRANDMOTHER *listens to them, then begins her story:* Well, once there was a wicked king, who didn't like cold weather; so he sent his soldiers, and told them to catch all the cold Wind Fairies and—

TOM *interrupts her to ask:* Are there really Wind Fairies, Grandmother?

GRANDMOTHER *answers:* Of course there are. I think I heard them a moment ago. Listen!

They all listen. The Wind Fairies are heard outside, like this:

z—z—z z—z—z z—z—z—z—z—z—z

Do you hear them? *asks GRANDMOTHER. The children all nod.* Yes, *she continues, going on with the story,* the king told his soldiers to catch all the Wind Fairies, and all the Snow Fairies, and Jack Frost himself, and to lock them all up in prison.

And did the soldiers do it? *asks HELEN.*

Yes, *answers GRANDMOTHER.* They locked up all of them except one little Wind Fairy, and he was so small and so quick, that they couldn't catch him; and what do you suppose he did? He rattled the windows so hard that the king couldn't sleep, and he blew so hard down the chimney and through the cracks around the doors, that he blew out all the lights in the king's house, and gave the king such a bad cold in his head, that—

Here Grandmother herself sneezes. And the Wind Fairies are heard outside, like this:

z—z—zz—z—zz—Z—Z—Z—z—z—z

How the wind does blow tonight, *says* GRANDMOTHER. Children, it seems to me very cold in this room. *She looks around to see what makes it so chilly.* Why, bless me, she says, they have forgotten to light the fire. *She rises, the children also, and they all go toward the fire-place.* Frank, *says* GRANDMOTHER, hand me the matches. *He brings them. She stoops at the hearth, the children standing around, and soon a bright glow appears and is seen to dance about.* There, that will soon make a fine blaze, *says she.* Hold up your hands, children, and warm them.

But suddenly from up the chimney comes the voice of JACK FROST: Hello there, you people, put that fire out. *Grandmother and the children are startled.* Do you hear? *shouts* JACK FROST. Put it out. Santa Claus is coming. Do you hear what I say? SANTA CLAUS IS COMING. Put out that fire.

Why, children, *cries* GRANDMOTHER, I had forgotten all about that. Quick! We must indeed put the fire out at once. Ned, bring me that pitcher of water.

He brings it; she throws the water on the fire. The glow disappears and a great hissing sound is heard, loud at first, then dying away, like this:

S—S—S—s—s—s—s—s—s—s—s—s—s—s

There! says GRANDMOTHER. It is quite out, you see. And now, you must hang up your stockings, quickly, and hurry into bed. *A shrill whistle is heard outside.* What was that? GRANDMOTHER *asks.*

It sounded like a whistle out of doors, *answers* MARGARET; *and she goes to the window and looks out.* Why, Grandmother, *says she,* it's beginning to snow.

Good! says GRANDMOTHER. That will make it easier for Santa Claus to get here in his sleigh. So make haste with your stockings, and then, before you get into bed, we will read from the Good Book about what happened on the first Christmas night so many, many years ago.

They bring their stockings and hang them in a row over the fireplace. Meantime Grandmother has taken the big Bible, and seated herself in the low chair in the middle of the room. The children, when the stockings are hung, group themselves beside her, standing, looking over her shoulders, her arms around some of them. Then GRANDMOTHER *reads:*

And there were shepherds in the same country abiding in the field, and keeping watch by night over their flock. And an angel of the

Lord stood by them, and the glory of the Lord shone round about them; and they were sore afraid.

And the angel said unto them, "Be not afraid; for, behold, I bring you good tidings of great joy, which shall be to all the people. For there is born to you this day in the city of David a Saviour, who is Christ the Lord. And this shall be the sign unto you: Ye shall find a babe wrapped in swaddling clothes, and lying in a manger?"

And suddenly there was with the angel a multitude of the heavenly host praising God, and saying, "Glory to God in the highest, and on earth peace, good will toward men."

And it came to pass, when the angels went away from them into heaven, the shepherds said one to another, "Let us now go even unto Bethlehem, and see this thing that is come to pass, which the Lord hath made known to us."

And they came with haste, and found Mary and Joseph, and the babe lying in the manger.

Then GRANDMOTHER closes the Book. And now your prayers, says she.

They all kneel down for a few moments, the boys by the bed on the right, the girls by the bed on the left. Then they rise and climb into the beds.

But SALLY has a question to ask: May we sing one song, Grandmother, before we go to sleep?

And GRANDMOTHER answers, Well, just one.

Then sitting up in the bed, they sing the dear old song, that is called

THE CAROL OF CHRISTMAS NIGHT

Holy night! peaceful night!

All is dark save the light

Yonder where they sweet vigil keep

O'er the Babe, who in silent sleep

Rests in heavenly peace.

Silent night! holiest night!

Darkness flies; all is light!

Shepherds hear the angels sing,

"Hallelujah! Hail the King!

Christ, the Saviour, is here,

Jesus, the Saviour, is here."

When the song is finished, they all lie down. Grandmother tucks the bed-clothes about their shoulders, and goes out. Soon they are all asleep.

Then a faint sound of sleigh-bells is heard on the roof.

Then all is quiet for a moment.

And THEN Santa Claus comes down the chimney, and steps out into the room. Silently he looks at both beds, full of sleeping children, turning his pocket flash light on them, so as to see them better. He counts the children in each bed. Then he counts the stockings hanging by the fire-place to be sure they are all there. Next he fills each of the stockings, taking the toys out of his pack. Then he takes his empty bag, and, after looking once more at the children, he disappears up the Chimney.

And this is the end of the Play.

Characters And Costumes

MOTHER GOOSE—The conventional costume; full skirt, peaked hat, cane, spectacles, mits. It is effective for her to draw her lips tight over her teeth so that her speech is that of a toothless old woman.

JACK FROST—All in white, decorated with tinsel, tall peaked cap, white gloves.

THE CHIMNEY—No costume; for he sits inside the chimney throughout.

THE WIND FAIRIES—Four little boys, all in gray, capes, caps, half-masks, long stockings.

THE SNOW FAIRIES—Four little girls, all in white, capes or coats, hoods, muffs. The muffs full of loose cotton, which they use as snow, to hang on trees and chimney, and to throw at Santa Claus.

SANTA CLAUS—The conventional costume; white hair and beard; pack, with few toys protruding from the top.

THE GRANDMOTHER—Gray hair, lace cap, gray or black dress.

THE GRANDCHILDREN—Four boys in pajamas, with wrappers over them; four girls in night dresses with kimonos over them.

Scenery And Scenic Effects

SCENE I.

The Chimney, which must be large enough to hold two people, one of them Santa Claus with his pack of toys, may consist of a light frame covered with turkey red cambric and backed with cardboard or heavy paper. The cambric should be marked off into bricks. The face is produced by cutting away the cardboard or paper backing behind two bricks for the eyes, one for the nose and two together for the mouth. Boxes must cover these openings on the inside, one for each eye and a larger one for mouth and nose together. In these three boxes are three electric lights which can be turned on and off independently by the boy inside the chimney. Dry batteries have been used when an electric current was not available. The light shining through the cambric makes the face. Turning off, and on again, the light behind one of the eyes makes the chimney wink, etc. Small hooks or nails, sticking out above the eyes, under the nose, and under the mouth, should be provided to hold the snow which the fairies hang on to represent eyebrows, mustache and beard.

The background and flies for this scene should be made of black cambric, dull side out, and a dim light should be used, blue or green preferable, so distributed as not to throw shadows on the "sky."

The trees may be real spruces or pines, or may be painted, or may be made of green cambric touched up with paint or charcoal.

The wind noise is made by some one behind the scenes, preferably not the Wind Fairies themselves. It should be plainly heard. The same applies to the sound of water thrown on the fire.

If accompaniment is desired for the songs, a violin gives a better effect than a piano.

The effect of falling snow is produced by a simple machine, consisting of a connected series of perforated cardboard boxes suspended from a cord or wire, and filled with finely cut paper. At one end they are attached to a wire spring, and by a cord at the other end they are shaken, so as to make the paper snow shower down. Such a machine may be bought for a small sum from firms dealing in Sunday School supplies. Two of them used together are more adequate than one.

SCENE II.

It is not necessary to use real beds. Boards on low horses or boxes will make excellent substitutes, and a strip of cloth will conceal their structure. An advantage of this plan is that they need not be as long as regulation beds. Four children to a bed means packing them like sardines, but it can be done, and it always amuses the audience.

The effect of a fire on the hearth can be made by quick motions with an ever-ready flashlight operated from behind. The children and Grandmother, standing in front, allow but an imperfect view of the fire-place, so that the illusion is easy to produce. The fireplace, however, may be a real one, if that is more convenient. In that case the flashlight must be operated by one of the children, kneeling in front of the fire-place; and when Santa Claus enters the room must be absolutely dark, so that he will first be seen when he turns on his flashlight, as he crouches before the fireplace, having apparently just come down the chimney.

If candies or gifts are to be distributed to children in the audience, as when this play is used as the Christmas entertainment of a Sunday School, Mother Goose may come out again, as soon as the curtain closes after the second scene, and speak as follows:

Well, my dear children, my little Play for you is finished, and I hope you liked it. There is just one thing left to be said. Those little boys and girls whom you saw asleep in their beds found that Santa Claus had not only put into their stockings presents for THEM, but also left something for YOU; and what do you suppose it was? A box of candy for each one of you, and if you will sit still a moment longer, the curtain will open again, and the candy will be handed to you. And so, my dears, as I say Good-night, I wish you all (or I hope you have all had) a Merry Christmas and (wish you) a Happy New Year.

<u>1</u>

To the tune "*D' ye ken John Peel?*"

<u>2</u>

To the tune of Schumann's "*Kindernacht.*"

The End

www.ingramcontent.com/pod-product-compliance
Lightning Source LLC
Chambersburg PA
CBHW071347310526
45790CB00018B/1388